"Putting firefighters in front of fires like these is like putting a man in front of a blow torch."

—United States
Forest Service Spokesperson

Yellowstone's
RED SUMMER

Text and Photographs by Alan and Sandy Carey
Introduction by Peter Matthiessen

 Northland Publishing

Editor note: Some of the interviews that comprise
the "Wildfire" section of the book were edited and
paraphrased for length.

Book Design by Ruth Ann Border, Flagstaff, Arizona
Typography by Prepress Graphics, Flagstaff, Arizona

All photographs are by Alan and Sandy Carey
unless otherwise noted. The publisher wishes to
thank Robert Bower/*Idaho Falls Post-Register*
(pp. i, 27) and Jeff Henry (p. x) and Jim Peaco
(pp. 22, 33) of the National Park Service for
permission to reproduce their photographs.

FIRST EDITION

ISBN 0-87358-483-X

Library of Congress Catalog Card Number
88-43556

Manufactured in Singapore through Palace Press

10K/1-89/0210

*We dedicate this book to our parents—Doug
and Donna Carey and Tom and Lucille
Mayce—for their loving understanding and
support through the years.*

CONTENTS

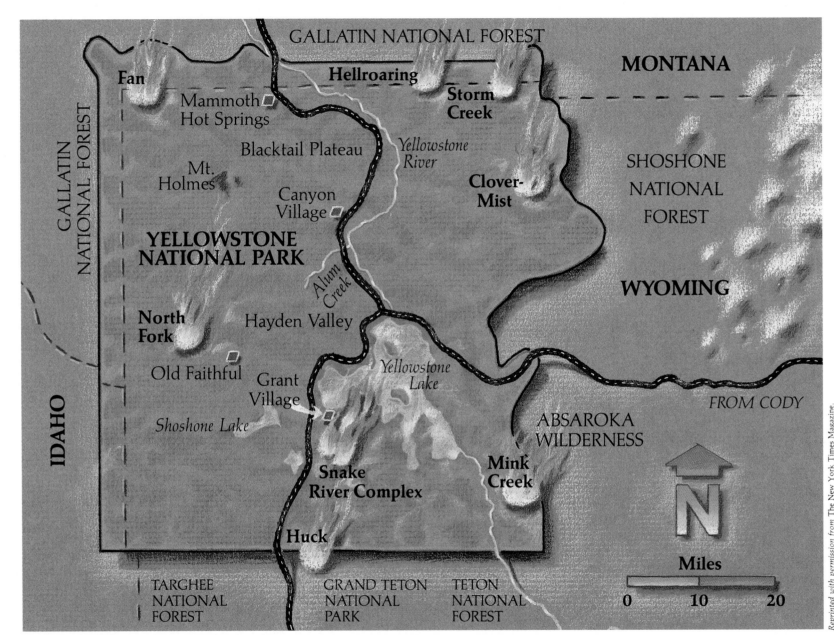

GALLATIN NATIONAL FOREST

MONTANA

Fan

Hellroaring

Mammoth
Hot Springs

Storm
Creek

Blacktail Plateau

*Yellowstone
River*

GALLATIN NATIONAL FOREST

Mt.
Holmes

Canyon
Village

Clover-
Mist

SHOSHONE
NATIONAL
FOREST

**YELLOWSTONE
NATIONAL PARK**

*Alum
Creek*

WYOMING

North
Fork

Hayden Valley

Old Faithful

Grant
Village

*Yellowstone
Lake*

IDAHO

Shoshone Lake

FROM CODY

ABSAROKA
WILDERNESS

Mink
Creek

Snake
River Complex

N

Huck

Miles

TARGHEE
NATIONAL
FOREST

GRAND TETON
NATIONAL
PARK

TETON
NATIONAL
FOREST

0   10   20

MAJOR FIRES THAT SCORCHED SECTIONS OF YELLOWSTONE NATIONAL PARK IN THE SUMMER AND FALL OF 1988.

STATISTICS

Yellowstone National Park: Established 1872 (the nation's oldest). 2,219,823 acres in Wyoming, Montana, and Idaho. Wildlife includes black and grizzly bears, moose, bison, and more than 225 species of birds.

Total firefighting cost: Approximately $115,000,000

Total acres burned: Approximately 1,000,000 within the boundaries of Yellowstone National Park.*

CHRONOLOGY

June 23   Red-Shoshone Fire
Lightning-caused. Started near a remote part of Shoshone Lake. Became a number-one priority fire on July 23, when it forced the evacuation of 3,000 visitors and employees from Grant Village. First introduction to the 200 hundred foot flames that would plague the firefighters throughout the summer. Later became part of the Snake River Complex fire.

June 25   Fan Creek Fire
Lightning-caused. Started on a ridge near Montana Highway 191, inside the western edge of Yellowstone. Became a number-one priority fire on August 2, as gusting winds pushed the flames across 16,000 acres. Finally contained in September after burning 23,000 acres. Completely extinguished in early November.

July 22   Clover-Mist Fire
Lightning-caused. Two small fires joined (Mist started July 9, Clover, July 11). Other small fires—Shallow, Fern, Raven, Sorrow, and Lovely—later merged with this fire as well. Devoured approximately 400,000 acres. Finally controlled in mid-October and completely extinguished November 13.

PERCENT OF NORMAL RAINFALL

	Apr	May	Jun	Jul	Aug
1977	10%	96%	63%	195%	163%
1978	91	126	42	99	46
1979	6	17	42	115	151
1980	33	152	55	143	199
1981	49	176	102	103	25
1982	169	74	89	118	163
1983	22	29	69	269	88
1984	44	84	66	297	121
1985	42	93	44	160	84
1986	145	47	64	212	75
1987	42	144	72	303	122
1988	155	181	20	79	10

Anticipating the continuation of this pattern, park managers and fire behavior specialists expected that natural fires could be allowed to burn. Six consecutive years of significantly above-average July rainfall suggested that July of 1988 would be similarly wet.

July 22 North Fork Fire

Man-caused. Threatened Old Faithful, Madison, Canyon, Norris, Mammoth Hot Springs, Tower-Roosevelt in the park itself, as well as the town of West Yellowstone. This fire, the "Brain" as some called it, had an uncanny way of finding and intimidating almost all of the main structures of Yellowstone. From the beginning, it was unpredictable and extremely hot. The heat generated at the time it approached Old Faithful was estimated to have been enough to heat 4,300 homes for one year, or three trillion BTUs of energy. On September 2 it was just one-and-a-half miles from West Yellowstone and residents were advised to keep their gas tanks full and their bags packed. This fire also caused the evacuation of park headquarters at Mammoth as well as the town of Jardine, Montana. Finally controlled by the first of November and completely extinguished by November 13. (See Wolf Lake Fire for the rest of the story.)

Late July Snake River Complex Fires

By this time, there were so many fires burning throughout the park that it was becoming very difficult for park officials to co-ordinate them. At this point, all of the southern complex fires—Red, Red Shoshone, Fall Mink, Factor, Continental, Badger, and Ridge—were categorized under one heading, Snake River. These fires were responsible for the closure of the park's entrance during most of August, and total acreage burned was approximately 225,000. Contained in mid-September and completely extinguished November 13.

August 15 Hellroaring Fire

Man-caused. Believed to have started with a cook stove in an outfitter's camp east of Gardiner, Montana. More bear incidents were reported on this fire than on any other. Burned approximately 83,000 acres before it joined with the Storm Creek Fire. Contained in mid-October, completely extinguished in early November.

August 20   Huck-Mink Fire

   Lightning-caused Mink started July 11 in the Teton Wilderness; Huck started
   August 20 when a tree fell on a power line. Caused the evacuation of the
   Flagg Ranch and campgrounds and the closure of Rockefeller Jr. Memorial
   Highway, which links the Grand Tetons to Yellowstone. Burned approxi-
   mately 225,000 acres. Contained in mid-September and completely
   extinguished November 18.

August 24   Wolf Lake Fire

   The man-caused North Fork Fire became so enormous that co-ordinating
   the firefighting efforts was too large a task for one commander;
   the northern section was split off and given a new name and new commander. These two fires burned over 500,000 acres. By September, the Wolf
   Lake fire section joined Clover-Mist, blighting the land with blackened trees
   and scorched ground from the park's eastern boundary to its western edge.
   Contained in mid-October, completely extinguished November 13.

Of these seven major fires, five burned into the park.

*The total burned acreage, as well as that listed for individual fires, represents approximate perimeter
totals. Fire burns in a patchwork pattern, attacking some areas while missing others. This type of
burning can result in lower figures for actual burned acres than the figures would, on the surface, indicate.

SCARVES WERE PROTECTION AGAINST THE ALL-PERVASIVE SMOKE.

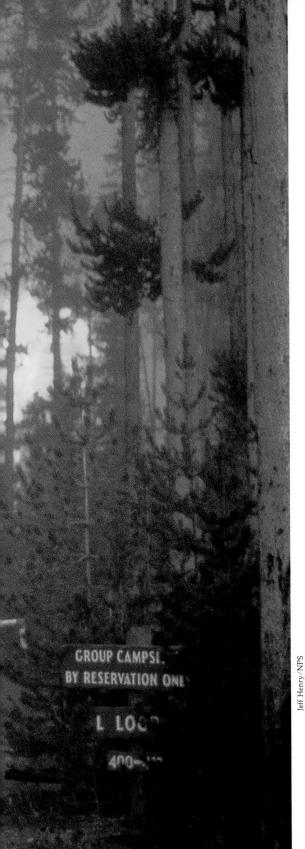

Jeff Henry/NPS

A SEASON OF FIRES

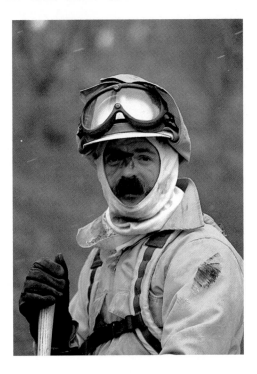

O
n August 17, 1886, Captain Moses Harris, in command of fifty men from the First United States Cavalry, arrived in Yellowstone National Park to take over management of the area, a function the army would perform for the next thirty-two years. Captain Harris (who had been appointed superintendent) and his company of soldiers did not have much time to ease into their new job: forest fires burned in scattered sections of the park and the soldiers were immediately transformed into firefighters. Captain Harris noted the following in a report on the situation:

> "I regret to have to report that destructive forest fires have been raging in the park during the greater portion of the present season. The most destructive one, which was burning when I arrived in the park, originated on the 14th of August last, near the east fork of the Gardner River, in full view from the Mammoth Hot Spring hotel and about seven miles distant. This fire is still burning, and has extended over a tract of country some ten or twelve miles in length by three to five in width."

> (from Aubrey L. Haines, *The Yellowstone Story*, volume II)

One hundred and two years later, on August 27, 1988, five hundred and fifty United States Army troops from Fort Lewis, Washington, arrived in Yellowstone to aid the beleaguered firefighters, who were frustrated by the seemingly unstoppable group of wildfires that had been running out of control for weeks.

It seems only appropriate that the army was in Yellowstone at a time when the towering flames were once again raging through this venerable jewel of the National Park Service system. In many ways, the park was a combat zone—the charred and burning shell of the forests, the smoky haze permeating the air, the heady sense of danger and excitement. Through the foul-smelling mist moved long lines of yellow-shirted men, their faces blackened and covered with sweat. But in this combat zone, men were not dying, the forest was; the soldiers and civilians fighting carried shovels, not rifles; planes dropped retardant, not bombs; and the sound of tracked vehicles came from bulldozers, not tanks. The tension was similar, however, because the foe was like an unstoppable, unreasoning army.

ARMY CHINOOK HELICOPTERS PROVIDED MUSCLE IN EQUIPMENT TRANSPORTATION.

Relentless and unpredictable, it attacked with amazing speed; advanced slowly; and, responsive to fickle wind direction, outflanked and surrounded its opposition. Many times during the long fire season, it would seem to fade in the morning and lull its opponents into a false sense of security, then rise in the afternoon with renewed vigor and strength. "The fires were like the return of Godzilla," one area commander noted. "All it took was a little wind and they resurrected themselves."

For all of man's ingenuity, he was almost helpless against this foe, for it was nature who brought it and in the end, only nature could defeat it. In the end, it had its season: Yellowstone's red summer.

ARMY FIREFIGHTERS DISEMBARK.

THE CASE FOR BURNING

*F*rom Cody, Wyoming, the road west to Yellowstone National Park follows the North Fork of the Shoshone River. Despite faltering rain in recent weeks— it was late October, and a fine fall morning, with the crowns of the last green cottonwoods turning to gold—a sign at the edge of the Shoshone National Forest read "FIRE DANGER." Of the national forests that surround Yellowstone— Shoshone and Bridger-Teton, to the east and south, in Wyoming; Gallatin, to the north, in Montana; and Targhee, to the west, in Idaho—the Shoshone was burned as much as any in the great fires of last summer. But there was no sign of the Clover-Mist fire that in late August escaped eastward from Yellowstone—one of great fires that made up what Yellowstone officials called "the most significant political, ecological, and economic event in the park's 116-year history."

Nor was there any blackened forest on the north shore of Yellowstone Lake, although its southern and western sides had burned entirely. Geese, widgeon, and mallard dabbled near the shore in the blue water, and a sleek gold-and-silver coyote, leaving a scent mark, worked the edge of a pine meadow near the lake.

Where the Yellowstone River departs from the great lake at its north end, bright bufflehead and Barrow's goldeneye swam in the sunlit river, a late osprey perched in a high tree, a rough-legged hawk in the uncommon dark phase flying overhead was noticeably fat. Hawks and owls fare well in time of fire, which exposes their prey and brings them hurrying from many miles away.

I took the road north toward Yellowstone Falls, passing calm bison at the wood edge, and still there was no sign of fire. Soon the green walls of lodgepole pine opened out in the broad mountain plains of Hayden Valley. Off this main road, three or four miles to the west, lay what was left of the old garbage dump along Trout Creek, where one summer twilight back in 1957 I watched the grizzlies come in across the sage, scattering the innumerable black bears. I eventually counted thirty-seven grizzlies in view at one time, sniffing at my old convertible, brawling, overturning burning barrels, in one of the most astonishing sights I have ever seen.

On the mountain prairie by Alum Creek was a herd of several hundred bison, and beyond the creek, along the northwest side of Hayden Valley, the black wall of the North Fork fire. Accidentally started by a woodcutter in Idaho's Targhee Forest on July 22, it went on to become the largest of the fires and the only one not yet "contained"—surrounded by firelines—by October 19, the day of my arrival. On the west side of the road, to Canyon Village and beyond, most trees still standing were black limbless spires, with burned-out logs on bare black earth. A pervasive stench of rain-soaked ash was disagreeably sweet and harsh at the same time.

Here in this scene of desolation, my assumption that the National Park Service must be at fault—whetted at the time of the grizzly controversy and intensified in recent years down in the Everglades—began to undergo a cautious change. I saw no sign of contented elk chomping new green shoots in the blackened forest, as suggested by recent news releases, but this stark scene seemed far less dreadful than press accounts of 200-foot-high flames, charred moonscapes, and fleeing citizens had me prepared for. It looked as if high winds had caused the flames to rush here and there in finger patterns, leaving countless patches of green forest within the outer perimeters of each fire. Even in places of most awesome burn, one was never out of sight of live green trees, which would very soon reseed these blackened areas.

Instead of gloom at the seeming "loss," the vast charred prospect, there came instead a heady sense of the earth opening outward, of mountain light and imminent regeneration, which made me recall how oppressive I once found the south part of the park, with its monotone enclosing stands of lodgepole pine. Far from being stunned by the destruction, I felt an exhilaration and relief, as if Yellowstone Park, for the first time in a century, had gotten a deep breath of fresh air.

Yellowstone, founded in 1872, from the beginning was America's greatest wildlife park. The definition of wildlife was selective. In 1916, the newly created National Park Service took over and joined with a will the national crusade against all predators and other "vermin," to protect the park's most eye-catching inhabitants, the elk and bison. By 1926, the native wolves were gone and the

cougar reduced to a few scarce fugitives in the northern mountains. In the absence of Indian hunters and predation, the sheltered ungulate herds overbrowsed their upland range, especially the aspen shoots and willow, which are relied on extensively by beaver as well.

The first stirrings of modern ecological thought emerged in the 1930s, when predator control—destroying "bad" animals to protect "good" ones—became suspect. A little late, the Park Service decreed that "no native predator shall be destroyed on account of its normal utilization of any other park animal, excepting if that animal is in immediate danger of extermination, and then only if the predator is not itself a vanishing form." This was the seed of the now-controversial policy of "natural regulation," which the park would apply to wildfires as well as animals. Yet as early as the 1930s, despite park policy, some "surplus" elk and bison were eliminated. In 1956–57, several thousand elk—half the northern herd—were slaughtered or removed to save their deteriorating range.

Present philosophy, which affirms the hands-off ideas of the '30s, stems from the so-called Leopold Report of 1963 (after A. Starker Leopold, who headed a distinguished panel of ecologists). It was narrowly interpreted by certain parks to justify strict "natural regulation," although the report itself was flexible, recommending not only encouragement of native predators but direct intervention, such as herd reduction to the capacity of the range.

But herd cropping in the mid-1960s met with such violent protest from both nature lovers in the park and eager hunters just outside it that Yellowstone took shelter in its present course of letting the park animals tend to themselves while devoting most of its attention to the two million large mammals who come by car from across the country every year.

What is good for multitudes of humans is rarely good for wildlife conservation. Grizzly and beaver were already in sharp decline.

In the late '60s, preferring the dull onus of overgrazed range to headlines about cruel slaughter of wild animals, the park began to "monitor" rather than manage the resurgent herds of elk and bison. It also continued to suppress all fire, although ecologists expressed alarm about the buildup of dead fuel wood in the forests. In 1972, responding to the urgings of conservation organizations, Yellowstone initiated a policy of "natural burn," which permitted wildfires started by lightning to burn themselves out except where they threatened the works of man. It resisted the idea of "prescribed burning," in which certain areas would be burned under controlled circumstances—in short, land management, which was anathema to the park philosophy of every organism (except the tourist) for itself. In recent years, the park's shamefully inadequate scientific research, according to one indefatigable critic—Alston Chase, author of *Playing God in Yellowstone*—has amounted to less than two percent of a budget dedicated to visitor comfort and protection.

"Natural burn" met its first real test in the dry year of 1979, when a number of lightning fires went along unmolested. The next year, an infestation of the pine-bark beetle added many more trees to the buildup of storm blowdown and dry fuel. In the early 1980s came a drought of seven years that intensified sharply after 1985. Unusually wet springs and summers were unable to offset thin snow packs, which lowered water levels and dried out the land. Then came a record drought year, 1988, when a meager snow pack and a wet spring followed the pattern, but dry, hot, windy summer days did not. The summer of 1988 had the lowest rainfall recorded in the park since 1876, the dusty year of Custer's death on the Little Bighorn. Drought and wind together brought about the million-acre accident that, according to park critics, had been waiting to happen for a hundred years.

On June 23, a lightning fire started at Shoshone Lake, in the southwest, and on June 25 what became the Fan fire was reported in the northwest corner of the park. In the next weeks, six other smoke plumes rose from the dark conifers to the blue sky. Because all but two (the North Fork and Hellroaring) were lightning fires, all but two were allowed to burn. Not until after mid-July, when the Shoshone fire and the Fan were already large, and the Clover fire (which had joined the Mist in the northeast) was a good deal larger, did park officials attack the Shoshone, mostly because it had come too close to the park community of Grant Village. People fearing a loss of tourist business were already saying that after three years of low rainfall, the park should have recognized the drought and acted earlier. On July 21, responding to howls of catastrophe from the public and its election-year politicians, park officals suspended "natural burn" indefinitely, in favor of the greatest firefighting effort in United States history.

Those anxious to blame the park for acting too slowly on these great fires might consider that the greatest of them all, the North Fork fire, was fought from the very start. "We threw everything at that fire from Day One," Denny Bungarz, a North Fork fire boss and veteran from Mendocino National Forest, said at the time. Things got so out of hand that the northeast section of this blaze, for tactical purposes, was considered a separate fire, the Wolf Lake.

THE FIRES WERE FUELED BY ACRES OF DEAD-AND-DOWN TIMBER.

Dan Sholly, Yellowstone's chief ranger and an expert firefighter, was an "incident commander," as fire bosses are now called, of the Wolf Lake fire. At his house in Mammoth Hot Springs, this husky squinting man—he lost his right eye in Vietnam—smiled ironically at that title. "These days," he said, "what you and I would call one hell of a high wind is called a 'wind event.' We had a lot of 'em. In the history of U.S. fires, the single factor that has made things most serious is wind."

Last summer, the wind scarcely diminished at night, carrying embers across the widest natural firebreaks, such as canyons and rivers. "We saw smoke convection columns like atomic mushroom clouds, 40,000 feet high!" Sholly said.

"We were criticized for not bulldozing firebreaks to slow the North Fork fire early," he told me. "But at that time the fire was fifteen miles from West Yellowstone, with no threat to property. It's not like Santa Monica, where you destroy everything to save million-dollar homes. Anyway, I doubt if 'dozers would have done much good.

"Not all of the outside crews understood that. The early crews, which we briefed ourselves, were aggressive where necessary but light on the land, but some of the later ones wanted cat [bulldozer] lines right and left, and complained that their hands were tied. This was true especially on the Clover-Mist, which escaped into the Shoshone National Forest, where the Forest Service wanted to protect its timber leases. The rules were different on each side of a boundary that the fire itself paid no attention to."

By mid-August the firefighting crews gained some control, but a "wind event" on the 19th was followed on August 20, "Black Saturday," by forty-to-sixty mile-per-hour gales, with gusts still higher, and in that twenty-four-hour period 165,000 acres went up in fire. "We couldn't hold any of the fire lines," Sholly said. "It was truly awesome."

Most of the park villages were closed August 24, and several of the gateway villages were evacuated in early September. From the first light rain on September 10 —the turning point—until heavier rain and snow a few days later, the park was closed.

FIRE WEAKENED AND BURNED THE TREES, WIND SNAPPED THEM OFF.

While at Yellowstone I made a two-hour flight over the park, with Project Lighthawk, an association of conservationist pilots. "We have to save some of this stuff," I was told by the young pilot, Gary Watson, who had flown down that morning to Gardiner, Montana, from Billings. The other passengers were Renee Askins, a wildlife biologist with the Wolf Fund, an education organization based in Moose, Wyoming, dedicated to restoring the wolf to Yellowstone, and biologist Frank Craighead's son Lance, a graduate student in conservation biology at Montana State University at Bozeman. Craighead, a bearded, cheerful fellow in round glasses who has hiked most of the park, served as our guide.

On Blacktail Plateau, off to the east, rose a line of isolated smokes from the North Fork fire. Around Mount Holmes, broad plateaus blackened by that fire stretched away for miles. Directly ahead lay the gateway community of West Yellowstone, which the North Fork fire approached within half a mile before bulldozers were brought in to gouge a fire line.

We proceeded south to the Old Faithful geyser basin and the Old Faithful Inn—a huge tinderbox saved from the North Fork fire on September 7, it is said, by its immense parking lot.

To the south lay the great burn called the Snake River fire and, in the distance, the snow peaks of the Tetons. Headed east again, we crossed the ochre meadows of Hayden Valley, which had survived unburned. Spotting the outline of the old Trout Creek dump, I boasted of my thirty-seven grizzlies, only to have Lance Craighead say, "The most I ever saw down there was eighty."

We flew out across the Shoshone National Forest, then turned north again, over steep canyons and the wild roadless country of grizzly and scarce bighorn sheep and cougar. Here andesitic, or granitic, soil supports spruce and fir as climax forest, and also the pale round whitebark pine whose nut crops fatten the bears for the long winter.

SMOKE PLUME OVER WEST YELLOWSTONE, MONTANA—A PORTENT OF WHAT WAS TO COME.

We rounded Pilot Peak on the east side and picked up the northeast entrance road into Cooke City. This gateway community, evacuated twice in early September, was threatened by flames from the Storm Creek fire, which started in the Custer National Forest of Montana and later joined the great Hellroaring fire in the Absaroka-Beartooth Wilderness. In the high winds in these mountains, the Storm Creek and Hellroaring fires once traveled in different directions on the same day. Neither penetrated nearly as deep into the park as the North Fork. Like all but three of the main fires—the Fan, the Clover-Mist, the Snake River—these two started outside the park, although they are lumped in the public's mind as "the Yellowstone fire." ("Whoever heard of Targhee National Forest?" says Dan Sholly. "The public and the press don't want to be confused by the real facts—it's so much easier to blame everything on the parks.")

Headed back west, the light plane left the road to cross the roadless northern section. On a high meadow, herds of elk and bison moved slowly. Gary Watson picked up the Yellowstone River again, and followed its Black Canyon down to Gardiner. Before parting, I asked Frank Craighead's son if he'd ever considered working with the park, because he knew Yellowstone so well. Lance smiled cheerfully and said, "It's hard to work with the Park Service if your name is Craighead."

Don G. Despain, research biologist and plant ecologist at Yellowstone, is devoted to all aspects of this mighty landscape, and as we drove to the burn on the Blacktail Plateau he discussed spruce budworm, mountain pine beetles, and other fascinating ecologic factors. "There's so little we really know," he said, all but rubbing his hands, as if he could hardly wait to find out more.

We walked respectfully through the black forest, in char stench and the requiem squawks of ravens. Using his jackknife, Despain dug up a tuft of grass and cut it to demonstrate how the passing fire had penetrated only a half-inch, leaving the root crowns still intact. "Over most of the area, the flames went through quickly and the burn was light. This black ground absorbs more sunlight and it warms up faster, and now it's fertilized with ash." He expected a quick return of grasses and heartleaf arnica, fireweed, and other deep-rooted plants.

All around were the burned cones of lodgepole pines, which require the heat of forest fires in order to open and release the winged seeds that scatter on the wind. The myriad seeds were already in place, and he picked up one of the wings to demonstrate how it contracts as it dries and expels the seed. The bases of the burned cones were still intact, a shining pewter gray.

Ash-dusted buffalo chips and gray-blue elk pellets, gold aspen leaves blown in from elsewhere, a gray spider crossing the black ground, unscathed. "Fire-resistant bark," Despain said with a slight smile, pointing at the stark skeleton of a Douglas fir, black cones still clinging to its bony branches, against a smokeless sky.

On all sides were fresh badger holes and the mounds of pocket gophers, both of which were well insulated from the fires. But the mice and moles were probably hard hit, because the leaf litter they depend on for their cover was gone, making them easy prey for the raptors and coyotes. "I once saw a nutcracker take a mammal," Despain said as that bold black-and-white bird, which usually eats seeds and insects, flew across the clear fall light between black snags. "Swooped in and picked up a mouse we'd just tagged for a mouse study, flew it right over to a tree." He looked happy to see me so astonished by nutcracker lore.

Everywhere on the black ground were tracks of elk and deer and coyote. Wolves were "the missing piece" in the whole ecosystem, Despain said, though he doubts if a few wolves would have much impact on the elk, a fecund creature that can multiply from 4,000 to 10,000 animals in a few years.

In a hollow was a grove of aspen, mostly unburned. For a new grove to establish itself, the seed must remain wet for two weeks and grow without any competition, conditions rarely occurring in the wild. Instead, new aspens sprout profusely from an underground runner system, and the new shoots are important forage for large animals. Like most aspen and willow in the park, these shoots had been damaged by overcropping.

Despain tends to attribute the decline of the aspen not to the alleged overabundance of the elk but to incompletely understood ecological factors. He also believes that the black bear, though now scattered, are as common as they were when their gangs cajoled the tourists at every corner. (Frank Craighead, whom I visited a few days later, says he does not believe this is true.) In these

AFTER THE FIRE WENT THROUGH.

ideas he has little more support from most biologists than he does for his optimistic view that even with the forage loss to drought and fire the large elk herd might adapt itself quite well to a hard winter. He thought it possible that the elk would move to different areas, use different foods.

"We don't know as much about ecology as we think we do," Despain said, waving his hand at the great prospect of forest and mountain rivers. "It's ecological arrogance to say that we should go out here and manage this—crop the herds, pre-burn the forests, manipulate Mother Nature, with some idea that everything can be kept just as it was. Impossible! Everything keeps changing,

the climate, the animal cycles. The pine bark beetle, beaver, aspen—everything comes and goes!"

Despain shook his head. "Our critics say we could have stopped some of those early fires, and it's true. Whether that would have made a difference once the rest got going, I doubt very much. The wind and heat built up air currents like small tornadoes, and big embers would fly out ahead, which torched off the next section. This North Fork fire was a natural force, like a volcano or a hurricane. Even when there was no wind, it rumbled like a locomotive, and when the gales came it sounded like a jet plane taking off. It came in from Idaho and did what it was going to do, and there was nothing we could do about it.

"As early as the 1930s, a plant ecologist named George McDougall spoke sharply against suppression of all fires, but it was some time before we heeded his advice, and by the time this bad drought came there was quite a buildup of 'down fuel' on the forest floor. Some people blame that on the spruce budworm, or the pine beetle—we call them 'infestations,' though they've probably been here a lot longer than the grizzly—but the intensity of the crown fire was offset by the insects' thinning effects on the tree crowns."

Despain has been studying the effect of burn and regeneration since 1974, and feels that one great benefit of these fires will be an immense amount of new information and research. "One day this summer when some trees torched right near where we were working, and flying embers ignited one of my nine plots, I was so excited about my experiment that I hollered out, 'Burn, baby, burn!' The press got wind of this and published it as the park's real attitude about the fire...and I wasn't allowed near a reporter for two months."

Asked about reports that the fire destruction might require 300 years to heal, Despain said: "The totally burned areas were mostly old forest of spruce and fir, or mature lodgepole. It might take three centuries for a given patch to go from black ground to mature lodgepole, then climax forest. But from an ecological point of view, there is no damage, there's still a forest ecosystem out there, nothing this park was established to preserve is lost. Dead trees may be a loss to house builders, but not to woodpeckers."

AN ASPEN GROVE BURNS.

Don Despain's optimistic point of view is generally shared by his Park Service colleagues, all the way up to the director, William Mott. "Fire is a stimulant and is as important to the ecosystem as sunshine and rain," the Yellowstone superintendent, Robert Barbee, told the press in late July. "This is not destruction—period!" he said later, an attitude in no way shared by politicians, nor by the public in general.

"These three states are all in economic decline, and tourism is very important; the tourism and travel people have a lot of clout with the politicians," Barbee said. "As soon as it pinches a little, they will start to holler, and the media will blow that up. Shove a microphone into somebody's face who's scared he's going to lose his house and say, 'The Government thinks this fire's a wonderful thing—what do *you* think?!' " He shook his head. Barbee is a big, genial, ruddy man, who after the most trying summer of his life has not quite lost an ironic sense of humor.

Donald P. Hodel, Secretary of the Interior (which includes and supervises the National Park Service), at first supported what the press (but not the park) had named the "Let-Burn Policy," but on September 10, when he escorted a delegation of Montana and Wyoming politicians and Richard E. Lyng, Secretary of Agriculture (which includes and supervises the United States Forest Service), on a tour of the fires, he appeared to be wincing from the heat. By early October, Hodel was calling the fires a "disaster" and expressing interest in a complete review of firefighting policies, reforestation and a program to feed the needy elk.

Wallop, citing the million acres already "lost" in the Yellowstone area, derided the let-burn policy as "absurd," and was joined by his Senate colleague, Simpson, in a demand for Mott's scalp. ("I had warned Bill Mott not to seem quite so enthusiastic about the fires, but he didn't listen," Barbee says.) Environmental groups generally defended Mott and dismissed Wallop's opinions as ridiculous, and the Republican Senators were accused of "head-hunting" by their Democratic rivals. Wyoming Governor Mike Sullivan declared ominously to the press: "Now is the time to get the fires out. We can kick butts later." Unquestionably, one of the menaced butts belonged to Barbee, who exclaimed to a reporter: "Why should I resign? This is a natural catastrophe. The myth that policy is responsible for this is just insane."

By mid-September, with cool damp weather, nine fires were still uncontained. No one mentioned the more than fifty that had been suppressed. Even the extent of the fires was debated. According to *Time* magazine (September 19), "the fires have ruined 1.2 million acres of Yellowstone and adjoining national forests." The day before, in *The New York Times,* Alston Chase mourned 1.5 million. But what most estimates were based on was the acreage enclosed by the fire perimeters —approximately 1.1 million acres, or one-half the area of the park. The forest actually burned was about half of that (perhaps one-quarter of the park) and the amount badly burned was about 22,000 acres, one percent of the park area, according to the park's chief research officer, John D. Varley.

Barbee himself has used the word "catastrophe," he told me, because of the human anguish and expense—at latest estimate, $120 million in the park alone. "We can't celebrate *that.* But from an ecological point of view, the fire was good for Yellowstone and for its wildlife. It is also of immense educational and scientific value in potential studies of recycling and diversity. Yellowstone is not fixed in formaldehyde and should not be fixed in time. It was *born* in cataclysm! These fires will make it a far more exciting place."

The creatures hardest hit by the fire were birds and small mammals—most critically, the porcupine and the rare pine marten. The remains of only a few hoofed animals, other than elk, have been located in daily helicopter surveys; no grizzlies were lost, and just one black bear. According to a count made by a park biologist, Frank Singer, on October 23, only 230 or 240 elk, out of 20,000 or more, died during the fires, all of them from smoke inhalation. What concerns Singer more is the loss of perhaps a third of the elks' winter range. Elk mortality in the event of a hard winter might come to 7,000 or 8,000 animals, but Singer, like John Varley, is philosophically opposed to artificial feeding, even in the event of heavy die-off—"what scientists call a 'significant perturbation of the animals,' " Bob Barbee said, teasing Varley. "Not one knowledgeable authority I've ever talked to supports artificial feeding," Varley said.

"The point is, nobody wants feeding except for the uneducated public," Barbee said, "and the media can fan the sentiment, just like the fires: 'First They Burn Down All the Forests, Now They're Starving Elk!' That's what they did when we tried to be straight with them, and notified them about one elk herd that was lost to smoke inhalation: 'Park Admits Mass Elk Mortality'—something like that." He gave me a wry look. "Media control might work better than fire control—don't answer their questions, just educate 'em, tell 'em what they ought to know."

The Greater Yellowstone Coalition, like Audubon, the Wilderness Society, and other conservation groups, generally supports present park policy. And Ed Lewis, its executive director, on his way through Mammoth to his home in Bozeman after attending a grizzly conference in Jackson Hole, was kind enough to

AIR FORCE TRANSPORT PLANE DISGORGES MARINE TRUCKS.

take the time to explain why. We sat in the sun at a picnic table outside the Yellowstone Museum, amid the barnyard smell and wistful bugling of hundreds of elk drifting into Mammoth on their way north to winter range. As they cropped the park lawns and stood about its headquarters, it was as if they were awaiting word about their fate.

Like most national parks, Yellowstone is not a complete ecosystem but an island of wilderness in which many species tend to disappear as their natural wanderings and migrations are cut off. Though Yellowstone and the much smaller Grand Teton National Park just south of here might be called the heart of it, they are only 2.5 million acres out of the 12 million to 14 million acres of the Greater Yellowstone Ecosystem, which includes about 10 million acres of national forest in the three surrounding states as well as nearly 1.5 million run by three national wildlife refuges, the Bureau of Land Management, and state and private interests. The large animals such as bison, elk, and grizzly, indifferent to park borders, are chronically in conflict with irate ranchers, ambitious hunters, and state agencies.

The G.Y.C., as it is known, was formed in 1983, out of concern for the hydra-headed administration of the Greater Yellowstone Ecosystem, which led policy in all different directions. The management of the grizzly (which Montana hunters would like to see removed from the endangered-species list) was similarly uncoordinated. As Ed Lewis says: "The fires made clear that Yellowstone Park and the surrounding wild lands are inextricably interdependent. The fires totally ignored man's boundaries, following the natural features that define this ecosystem, and they were fought by very different jurisdictions and philosophies.

"What are the alternatives to present policy? Prescribed burning? Most people who really know the park do not believe that the 40,000 to 50,000 acres necessary to offset an event like this summer's could be burned systematically each year. In the autumn, in a normal year, there is too much precipitation; in winter and spring there is just too much snow. In summer you might get a fire going, but once you do, you can't always control it. Anyway, the park's fire policy has been consistently misinterpreted; it's very flexible, and allows for prescribed burns.

"We certainly hope that all these hearings"—he rolled his eyes toward Jackson Hole, where an interagency panel (Forest and Park Service) on fire-management policies had begun meetings a few days earlier—"will not lead us back to the

Jim Peaco/NPS

22 *YELLOWSTONE'S RED SUMMER*

Smokey Bear days of complete suppression, back to the same unnatural fuel buildup, and fires of too great intensity. If all fires had been fought right from Day One, when they were small and slow, most of them could probably have been stopped, but it's very unlikely that the ultimate result would have been much different. The park made the right decision in not using bulldozers, which leave scars that last for a long time. The impact of the firefighting might have been worse than the impact of the fire.

"Charred areas will probably lead to erosion and sedimentation of the streams, and hurt the fisheries, though those streams should clear up in about two years. There's a definite impact on elk forage and the white-bark pine nut crop, but for the moment, all indications are that the large animals came out of it mostly unharmed. The grizzlies look fat and happy, they are fattening up for winter on elk carcasses, and there'll probably be more carcasses by spring."

In general, the Greater Yellowstone Coalition is a strong supporter of park policies and decisions, which might seem to support criticism that such private groups and the Department of Interior form a conservation establishment that tends to encourage Park Service stagnation. And surely, in this torrid summer, the widespread perception of bureaucratic bungling and coverups underlay the accusations that the park was whitewashing its "too little and too late" reaction to the fires. Its cheery ecological prognostications, in the early days, at least, seemed to ignore the human consequences.

"This was a very unpleasant place to be," Lewis reflected. "Unlike Mount St. Helens, which was quickly over, the fires went on for weeks and weeks and weeks, with stifling smoke and sore throats and anxiety, and tempers ran high. The park just wasn't sensitive to this in its public statements. It tried to make the fire a totally positive thing, and this was one reason there was so much anger."

Like most of Yellowstone's well-wishers, Lewis hopes that the Government review panels will support present park policies in their report, appeasing the public with such recommendations as "more consideration of weather trends" and perhaps "pre-suppression efforts," such as brush-clearing in the vicinity of buildings. He, too, is afraid of a hard winter that might cause heavy mortality in the elk herds, inviting grim news stories of starving elk wandering the snowy wastes of the ruinous fires.

Such stories would surely re-ignite the public outrage, and panic the political appointees of the new Administration into ill-advised elk-feeding programs and other programs destructive in the long term to the wildlife for which Yellowstone was first established. Once again, shortsighted politics would harm the long-term welfare of the great deer that even now, as we concluded our discussions, wandered trustingly among man's habitations in these shining mountains.

— PETER MATTHIESSEN

Excerpted from the *New York Times Magazine,* reprinted by permission.
Peter Matthiessen first visited Yellowstone National Park in 1957, researching *Wildlife in America.* His most recent book is *Men's Lives: Surfmen and Baymen of the South Fork.*

OUT OF CONTROL

*Y*ellowstone's red summer began in June, with an insignificant flame, probably sparked by lightning that found a bed of tinder-dry lodgepole pine needles in a remote section of the park. This first bolt, combined with those that followed and some careless human acts, initiated a conflagration that caught the attention of the nation and the world. During the summer of 1988, over fifty fires raged through the park and adjacent national forest land, and about one-half of Yellowstone's 2.2 million acres went up in smoke.

There have been few forest fires in this century in the United States that have equalled the intensity of those that swept through Yellowstone. Firefighters with decades of experience said again and again that they had never seen wildfires so unpredictable, or those that so consistently broke all of the rules of normal fire behavior. As a result, firefighters were continually frustrated in their efforts to control the blazes. Firelines, backbreakingly dug, seldom contained the marching walls of flame, which, driven by gale-force winds, jumped over roads, rivers, and canyons with a regularity that was terrifying. Nine thousand firefighters from across the United States—including special military detachments—could not stop its destructive force. Helicopters dumped 750-gallon bucket loads of water and airplanes dropped fire retardant by the ton, yet had only minimal effect.

By the middle of August, strong winds blew every few days, or several days in a row, which meant that it was beyond hope that the fires could be controlled. One of the firefighters observed that "there weren't enough resources in the world to go in and actually suppress the fires. [It] was a tinder box situation. . . ." By the end of August, eighty percent of the nation's trained firefighters were in Yellowstone and Montana. Despite enormous numbers of man-hours and machinery, wildfires continued to dominate the park. As a result, firefighters were forced into a defensive strategy, and saving lives, buildings, and other property became a

SMOKE PLUMES OVER WEST YELLOWSTONE.

priority. Firefighters were sent ahead to protect threatened structures; sprinkler systems were set up, buildings were sprayed with fire-proof foam; and combustible materials were cleared away. Sometimes, though, their efforts were not enough, and property was destroyed.

Ray Ross, a Bozeman, Montana, pilot who worked under contract with the National Forest Service and whose summer was spent flying over the park, had an aerial view of the situation. He observed, "These fires were beyond the capability of man to control." He was right—human effort could not quell Yellowstone's fires; it took two September snowstorms to finally provide firefighters with an edge against the flames. Even then, some of the fires continued to burn into November.

The effects and costs of the Yellowstone fires were astronomical. Large sections of forest were charred and otherwise devastated; blackened skeletons of trees stand as stark reminders of the consequence of out-of-control wildfire. The cost of fighting the blaze has been estimated at well over $100 million, which does not include the millions of tourism dollars lost. The small towns that border the park—Cooke City, Silvergate (both of which had to be evacuated), West Yellowstone, and Gardiner Mountain—depend heavily on this seasonal revenue, and the economies of these communities lost between thirty and forty percent of what they would have normally received during the summer season.

WHO WAS TO BLAME?

The extent of the fires and their location stimulated an equally heated controversy; punctuated by accusations and finger-pointing, attention was focused on the National Park Service and its now-famous "let-burn" policy. Competition between various news media also served to create a degree of sensationalism that sometimes

FOAM WAS USED TO PROTECT STRUCTURES.

confused the issues. As a result, the public was often left with the impression that all of Yellowstone National Park was devastated. For example, one network evening-news program, filmed during the height of the blaze, was narrated by a reporter who stood in an area that had been burned in 1983 and then reburned in 1988; the reporter intoned dramatically, "Tonight, this is all that is left of Yellowstone."

Politicians were also involved in the controversy; demands for congressional hearings, and even the resignations of Secretary of the Interior Donald Hodel, Director of the National Park Service William Penn Mott, and Superintendent of Yellowstone National Park Robert Barbee were made. Montana Senator Max Baucus said that park and forest service officials acted "naively and stupidly" in not fighting the fires earlier, and another Montana senator, John Melcher, called the fire policy "a fiasco."

Not all of the confusion can be blamed on the news media and the politicians, however. The National Park Service also contributed its share of disorder. As one reporter commented, "You could talk to three Fire Information Officers within the space of a half-hour and they would all tell you something radically different, not because they were dishonest but because they really didn't know."

There *were* frequent communication lapses, but when one considers the size and number of the federal agencies involved—National Park Service; National Forest Service and its firefighters from all over the country; the Bureau of Land Management; the states of Montana, Wyoming, and Idaho; the United States Army and Marines; plus various small firefighting contingents—it is not surprising that there was confusion. (While covering the fires ourselves, the only consistent information we received was from the West Yellowstone Command Center.)

Despite the confusion and debates, the issue can be realistically reduced to two central questions: What was the cause of the fires and why did they burn so much for so long?

DESPITE MEDIA UPDATES, RELIABLE INFORMATION ABOUT THE FIRES WAS HARD TO OBTAIN.

THE YELLOWSTONE FIRE
MANAGEMENT PLAN

Prior to 1972, fires in Yellowstone National Park were fought; none was allowed to burn. Fire was considered to be a destructive and unnecessary evil that charred beautiful stands of forested land and was harmful to wildlife—who can forget the popular admonition of Smokey the Bear: "Only you can prevent forest fires"? Beginning in the 1960s, however, a new attitude toward forest fires began to take shape as federal land managers, aware of the ecological benefits of fires, re-evaluated their policies. In 1972, Yellowstone parks developed a new fire plan.

Yellowstone's plan included provisions that allowed lightning-caused fires to burn unimpeded unless they threatened buildings or property; man-caused fires were to be extinguished immediately. Each fire was to be evaluated on a case-by-case basis. Undergoing revision and refinement since 1976, the plan had four goals:

1. To permit as many lightning-caused fires as possible to burn under natural conditions.

2. To prevent wildfire from destroying human life, property, historic and cultural sites, special natural features, or threatened and endangered species.

3. To suppress all man-caused fires (and any natural fires whose suppression was deemed necessary) in as safe, cost-effective, and environmentally sensitive ways as possible.

4. To resort to prescribed burning when and where necessary and practical to reduce hazardous fuels, primarily dead and down trees.

Ironically, revisions in the Yellowstone Fire Management Plan were in their final stage of approval in the spring of 1988.

Jim Peaco/NPS

It was the first goal of the plan that stimulated the heart of the 1988 controversy. This goal—allowing lightning-caused fires to burn under natural conditions—became known as the "let-burn" policy and was the target of the anger voiced by tourists, reporters, and citizens of West Yellowstone and Cooke City. The same refrain was voiced by all: "The rangers are letting Yellowstone burn and we want it stopped now." The logical consequence of goal one became a thorn in the side of Yellowstone's management team as the summer progressed.

In late June, though, there were no dramatic indications of the catastrophe to come; there had been twenty lightning-caused fires, eleven of which had self-extinguished. Park management and fire-behavior specialists saw no reason to anticipate that the 1988 season would be any different than those previously experienced. But by mid-July, the scenario had changed, and the potential for enormous problems began to become evident. Although April and May had been unusually wet, June and July brought almost no rainfall, and August continued that pattern. In retrospect, these three summer months went on record as the driest in the park's 112-twelve-year recorded history. Also by mid-July, the moisture content of grasses and small branches in the park was measured at as low as three percent; that of downed trees was seven percent. (In comparison, kiln-dried lumber has about a twelve-percent moisture content.) These levels were noted by Rod Norem, a park fire analyst, as the lowest in his twenty-two years of experience.

The hot, dry weather combined with the extremely low moisture content of the vegetation and strong prevailing winds caused the first stage of revision of the Fire Management Plan: no new fires would be allowed to burn, with exceptions being made for natural fires that started adjacent to existing fires. This meant that if a new fire appeared to meld with an existing fire, it would be allowed to burn. At the time of the July 15 revision, total acreage burned had reached 8,600; by July 21, weather conditions had not improved and the burned acreage had grown to 17,000 acres. (Prior to this time, the largest fire in Yellowstone's history was the Heart Lake fire, which in 1931 burned 18,000 acres.)

A RAPIDLY SPREADING BLAZE OCCUPIES TOURISTS' ATTENTION.

At this point, the Fire Management Plan was further revised to one succinct goal: "Put them out." By July 23, the situation had deteriorated further, as 200-foot walls of flames from the lightning-caused Red-Shoshone Fire forced the evacuation of 3,000 visitors and employees from Grant Village. On July 27, Secretary of the Interior Hodel, under increasing political pressure, visited Yellowstone and reaffirmed that the Fire Management Plan had been suspended and that all fires would be aggressively fought. Politically, the park was compelled to devote all of its resources to the fires, but realistically, it was too late. They were well into the siege of '88.

As the fires increased their force in August, so did media coverage, followed by increased attacks on Yellowstone's management plan. It was targeted as the primary reason for the damage to the park's forests and meadows, but in reality, about half of the total acres were burned by fires that had started outside of the park's borders.

BULLDOZING YELLOWSTONE: OPPOSING POLICIES

Another point of contention was Yellowstone's management decision to not allow bulldozers within park boundaries during the early part of the fire season. There were a number of critics, including some incident commanders, who complained that fire suppression efforts were being hampered by this restriction, as bulldozers can put in firelines much more rapidly and effectively than hand crews. These experienced firefighters believed that they could have drastically reduced the acreage burned had they been allowed the use of the big earth-moving machines in the initial stages of the fire.

The most classic example of this can be seen in the North Fork fire. This fire, first reported on July 22, burned almost 400,000 acres and threatened Old Faithful, Canyon Village, the Norris Museum, Mammoth Hot Springs, Tower-Roosevelt Lodge, and the community of West Yellowstone. Believed to have been started by a spark from a woodcutter's saw or cigarette, it was discovered southwest of West Yellowstone on the Targhee National Forest, about two hundred yards outside the park boundary.

Two Forest Service fire-prevention technicians, Jill Kelly and Jim Cox, were the first on the scene that afternoon. As Jill recalled, "When we arrived at the fire location about 2:30 PM, it had already burned about sixty acres and was 'cranking and rolling.' We called for assistance and were sent two bulldozers and four fire engines. We put in dozer lines from the origin of that fire up to both sides of the park line so that by evening, it was completely contained on our side of the Targhee National Forest."

Unfortunately, by this time, the fire had spread into Yellowstone National Park. When the Forest Service requested permission to use bulldozers inside the park boundaries, it was denied. Instead, hand crews were brought in to work on firelines. The firefighters worked—in vain—into the next day to control the fire, but the man-made lines could not hold it.

A decision was made to pull the crews off the North Fork fire, as it was considered low priority and its remote location was perceived to make it no immediate threat other than to the sea of dead trees ahead of it. At the same time, the Clover-Mist fire was threatening to escape Yellowstone onto national forest land, and the Red-Shoshone fire was menacing Grant Village. The latter two were classified as high-priority, and the majority of available resources were used in trying to control them. Another factor considered was that the crews committed to the North Fork fire were being subjected to unsafe conditions because of the fire's extremely unpredictable behavior. Given these circumstances, and given the odds, it was decided that it was pointless to keep the crew on the North Fork.

Two days later, the North Fork fire was off and running and heading straight toward Old Faithful. This once low-priority fire soon became the number-one interest in Yellowstone and remained in that position throughout most of the summer.

The $25 million question, then, is, if the Forest Service had been allowed to continue using bulldozers inside the park boundary that first afternoon, would they have been able to establish a fire line around the blaze that would have contained it? One Forest Service official, with years of firefighting experience, had this to say: "Based on past experience and similar situations, had we continued our fire suppression efforts on the North Fork fire with mechanized equipment into the park at that time, the odds were in our favor that we could have been successful in containing it."

As the fires grew in size and intensity and threatened major developments within the park, political pressure was brought to bear. As a result, by August, bulldozers *were* allowed within Yellowstone in a limited capacity. However, the nature of the fires—spot fires leaped consistently one-half mile and sometimes one mile ahead of the main fire fronts—defied everything, including the bulldozers. Larry Caplinger, incident commander for the North Fork fire commented that, "on the majority of these fires, bulldozers would have to be used along the flanks to be effective. The way they burned this year, any time you tried to crowd them, the lines got eaten up. There are a number of 'dozer lines in the park that are burned on both sides."

Bulldozers have been used extensively in fighting forest fires over the last few decades, and might have reduced the total acreage burned and perhaps even contained the North Fork fire in its early stages with a minimum of damage. There are consequences, however, as expressed by Denny Bungarz, a North Fork incident commander: "If I would have used bulldozers extensively when the fire was raging through the park, I might have been able to reduce the total acreage burned by 100,000 acres, but there would have been tracks all over the place." This

viewpoint was reinforced by a firefighter from Washington state, who mentioned a fire that had burned in his state twenty years ago and noted that, while traces of the fire had faded, the scars from the bulldozers were still glaring eyesores.

Yellowstone's Chief Ranger, Dan Sholly, was asked his opinion on the utility of fighting fires with bulldozers. "On the San Bernardino National Forest in southern California, there are hundreds of miles of bulldozer lines that were used as firebreaks along the foothills. That kind of destruction would not be acceptable in Yellowstone."

Because Yellowstone is managed primarily as a wilderness area, this level of mechanical destruction is not allowed in any but the most exreme circumstances. In a wilderness area, fire crews are directed to be "light on the line," to construct firebreaks that are minimally damaging to the land in order to preserve as much of the area's wilderness characteristic as possible. Forest Service areas categorized as "wilderness" also follow this policy; the Forest Service, however, has a multiple-use policy that allows them to manage their lands for logging, mining, grazing, recreation, and other more intrusive uses. Management of multiple-use lands is carried out under a different standard than is used for those designated as wilderness.

Two examples of the effects of these policies in Yellowstone were the North Fork and the Hellroaring fires. The former originated in a multiple-use area, and bulldozers were allowed up to the park's boundaries. In contrast, the Hellroaring started on the Gallatin National Forest in the Absaroka-Beartooth Wilderness

Area, and bulldozers were not utilized. Another example of the consequences of opposing policies can be seen in the beginning of the Clover-Mist Fire, which was suppressed on the Forest Service side of the boundary and allowed to burn on the park's side.

Although these differences created confusion among the general public as well as the firefighters themselves, and clearly helped fuel the controversy, the policies did not *cause* the fires. Whether or not they helped establish the conditions that allowed the fires to burn to the extent that they did has not been conclusively answered.

Yellowstone Superintendent Robert Barbee has been highly criticized for the way in which he directed the park's firefighting efforts. Hindsight indicates that different decisions may have had more positive results on the outcome. The decisions were made, however, under conditions seldom, if ever, previously experienced, and were within the limits of an established fire policy. Bureaucratic policies have as their cornerstone an insistence on working within policy framework, and so it is difficult to suggest how Superintendent Barbee, given this dictum, might have acted differently.

Review teams are investigating the fires as well as the fire policy. Through these investigations, it is hoped that the unanswered questions will be resolved and that the information collected will provide more effective guidelines in the event that similar situations develop in the future.

WILDFIRE

*B*y mid-August, conditions in the park were extreme. The whole area was extremely dry, as Rod Norem, an area command fire behavior analyst, noted. "The soils were so dry that there was practically no water in the soil-plant system. Fires normally slow down at night because of the rise in humidity, which in turn raises the moisture content of the fuels. In Yellowstone, even when the humidity got up to eighty percent or so at night, it was so dry that the fuel-moisture content only went up by one or two percent. Because of this, we had twenty-four hour burning periods. That put us in a whole new ball game.

"The probability of ignition during this period was well into the nineties; this means that when an ember lands on the ground, there is a ninety percent probability that it will ignite. When you're trying to fight a fire, fifty percent is considered alarming and anything above sixty percent is considered extreme."

From the Logbook . . .

Often, the most visceral view of the fires can be gathered from those actually involved with them. The firefighters recorded their observations, both philosophic and mundane, in a variety of camp logbooks, and their comments are excerpted here.

The smoke column from our fire is reaching elevations of 35,000 feet and can be seen in most of Montana, Wyoming, and Idaho.

Norem illustrated his point by the following example: "I was in an ember shower near a fireline and saw an ember land on a log. I watched it propagate out almost like sparklers catching, and burn a little round patch on that log. Shortly thereafter, it burst into a little flame. Experience tells you that you don't throw a stack of logs into a fire and expect it to burn, but it was just about twenty minutes from the time I saw the ember hit the log until it flamed up and was crowning out the trees above it. Those torching trees then cast their own embers ahead of them...that's how a fire moves."

Under these extreme conditions, the fires *did* move. The worst day was generally considered to be August 20, a Saturday, when the fires devoured over 150,000 acres. This was the greatest number of acres burned in any one twenty-four-hour period, and was terribly demoralizing to the firefighters as they watched the flames leap across the firelines they had worked so hard to put in. While no one was killed on that day, there were some narrow escapes.

Firefighters, hikers, and others left Yellowstone with a number of harrowing stories; following are a few of the more dramatic.

One of our first high-priority jobs was to get some toilet facilities set up. Slit trenches were the order of the day. The ground was rocky and holes were hard to dig. Finding a secluded place within walking distance was quite a challenge. And then, it takes more than one to serve everyone, and at the rate it is going, the fire will be out before we get enough trenches dug.

THE LOSS OF BULL MOOSE CABIN

Although the firefighters were able to save many buildings, a few burned, largely because of their remote location and the intensity of the fires. Unfortunately, one of those was the historic Bull Moose cabin in the Absaroka-Beartooth area. This cabin, built around 1908, had been used by back-country travelers, sheepherders, poachers, and a host of others for years; it had great sentimental value for area residents.

We made plans for the next day, ate some supper, and retired for the night. I slept in a box, which was quite an experience, and I swear it will be my last. It got down to twenty-four degrees and there was frost all over everything. Have you ever tried to get dressed in a box?

Dan Tyres, a resource advisor of the Hellroaring fire, witnessed the circumstances of the cabin's destruction. "On August 18, we checked the cabin to see if it could be protected from the fire. After determining that it could, we left. The same night, a spot fire that jumped to the west side of the Hellroaring drainage was noted, but that information was not effectively passed to the people working on the fire. The next day, firefighters working on the Hellroaring fire didn't immediately see this smaller fire because of all the smoke. When it was finally realized that the area was burning, they got over to it, but it was full of torching trees. The fire crew was forced to retreat when it began burning on both sides of them.

"A good wind behind it, the fire picked up momentum and made a run that put the Bull Moose cabin directly in its path. The fire went through the west fork like it was going through a chimney; there was nothing that could be done to stop it. If we'd put crews in front of the blaze, they would've been casualties. I saw flames torching water-rooted grass.

"The next day, I went back with a rehab team and found nothing but melted metal at the cabin site. A lot of emotion had been invested in that cabin—you could identify with the past through it. We all felt a great sense of loss."

Today was my birthday and we had a little party. I got a cake and a moose hat. Thanks!

INTO THE CREEK

On the morning of August 20, Tom Shorten of Billings, Montana; his German shepherd dog Chico; and three companions set out from Lulu Pass into the Absaroka-Beartooth Wilderness Area just north of Yellowstone for a three-day backpacking trip. Hiking cross-country to Anvil Lake, they made camp, and then Tom decided to take his compass and his dog and explore on his own.

"I had been hiking for quite a while when I noticed that it was becoming very smoky; the denseness of the smoke increased rapidly. I began to be a little anxious, and realized that I might be somewhere that I didn't want to be. As I was trying to get my bearings, a fire blew over the ridge. The heat, the wind, and the fire—it was amazing. Grabbing my dog, I ran blindly toward a nearby creek.

Trying to get facilities to put something at river crossing so crew won't have to wade river twice a day. Problems related to water, wet boots.

FIRE SWEPT ACROSS WATER, THROUGH FORESTS.

"Fortunately, I found a place where two large rocks had fallen together and made a cavelike space across the water; there was a small opening at the top where the rocks met. We dove in under this shelter and lay in about two feet of water—because of the drought, it wasn't very deep anywhere in that area. We lay there looking out; at that point, I wondered if we would make it. It became desperately hot and bright even though we were as far under the rocks as we were able to get. There was so much debris flying through the air and falling through the opening above us that my hair and clothes kept catching on fire.

"The wind created by the fire was unbelievable—I saw it take an apparently healthy eight-inch pine tree right out of the ground. That roaring wind sucked everything up. Then came the flames; they passed over us with the sound of a jetliner and moved down the creek. By then we had been in the water about forty-five minutes. The smoke was so heavy and thick that it was difficult to breathe; I was able to filter out some of the smoke by breathing through my shirttail, which I'd pulled up over my face, but my dog kept passing out.

"Although it was nighttime, it was as bright as day, and I watched the fire continue to burn down the creek and then cross the next ridge. As the brightness dimmed, I began to relax, then noticed that the roar of the fire was getting louder rather than more faint. The fire was coming back, and the sky began to lighten again...I was shocked, and felt that we might not survive this attack. Then, like a miracle, it hit a spot that had been burned earlier and shot off in another direction.

"We had been in the water for about three hours by this time, and finally the cold drove us out. We were both shaking violently, and although everything was still on fire and burning around us, we climbed on a rock in

A wind shift at about 9 PM blew the Storm Creek fire over the south containment line into the Lost Creek drainage due to heavy spotting. Crews were unable to stop the fire from spreading.

the water near a burning log and tried to get warm. We sat on that rock until daylight.

"When it was light enough to see, we started to head south through what seemed like miles and miles of devastation. There was nothing green in sight, and I was walking in six to eight inches of ash. I had to carry my dog most of the way—his feet were badly burned—and as a result, had to stop frequently to rest; we travelled this way for seven or eight miles, dodging falling trees. The knowledge that one could fall on us was almost as bad as being in the creek and watching the fire come back. By the time we reached Lulu Pass and my car, my shoes were just about burned off, my shirt was in tatters, and I was black from head to foot, but grateful to be alive.

"During the whole ordeal, I did a lot of praying, because I really didn't believe that I was going to make it. And I believe that I wouldn't be here now if it weren't for answered prayers. This happening turned into a personal kind of tragedy-triumph for me and I thank the Lord."

(LEFT) AFTER A FIRESTORM... (RIGHT) TREES WEAKENED BY FIRE WERE CONSTANT THREATS.

ON THE FIRELINE

Firefighting is a tough business—exhausting, hot, and dirty. Days spent
building a fireline can be wasted when it burns up in a matter of minutes.
Backbreaking work, long hours, sometimes short rations, and
uncomfortable nights sleeping on the cold ground are routine.
Smokejumper George Jackson, who spent 115 days on the Yellowstone
fires, said, "The fires got to be *too* much, a physical and mental strain."

*Fire suppression was very difficult
today, fireline that held for ten days
is now blowing out.*

JUMPING INTO THE FIRE.

Several supply drops by parachute were made and mostly arrived in good shape. One of the packages free-fell and didn't fare very well. It happened to be the carton that contained the first-aid supplies, rations, and lime. We had aspirin mixed with lime and lime mixed with rations. Needless to say, we had to dispose of nearly all of the contents.

Les Meade, an emergency medical technician from Billings, described some of his experiences. "I originally went to West Yellowstone for a fishing trip and ended up volunteering to work on the fires, treating firefighters. The hours were long, 5 AM to midnight, and medical supplies were short. One of the main problems that plagued the firefighters was burned and blistered feet. This was particularly common among the military firefighters, as their boots weren't heavy enough to insulate their feet from the hot ash and embers that covered the ground at two-to-six-inch-deep thicknesses.

"Another common ailment was respiratory problems caused by smoke inhalation. We gave fifteen-minute oxygen treatments, which speeded up the healing process and enabled the firefighters to return to the fireline more quickly.

"Fortunately, other than cuts (which were minor), there were very few serious injuries. I found this pretty incredible considering some of the dangerous situations these guys were in."

DENSE SMOKE WAS A HEALTH HAZARD.

OF MOOSE AND HELICOPTERS, BEARS AND MEN

For most of the firefighters working in and around Yellowstone, it was a unique experience to fight fires in an area that was home for large numbers and varieties of animals, especially large game animals. They seemed to enjoy seeing herds of elk and buffalo grazing in the high mountain meadows, sometimes quite close to the firelines.

The crew boss of Navajo 17 cautioned us today that he had smelled a dead animal north of the ranch; in grizzly country, that could attract trouble.

A military firecamp at Madison Junction was a beehive of activity, with firefighters and diesel trucks and buses continually moving in and out of camp. Yet a herd of elk and a few buffalo spent the entire summer in a meadow directly adjacent to the camp, seemingly oblivious to the commotion. However, this close association did lead to some problems. Both elk and buffalo have a habit of rubbing horns, antlers, heads, and bodies against anything that provides resistance. Trees, rocks, and buildings are their normal targets.

Helicopters have to be fenced at night to protect them from friendly bison.

When the object of this behavior was helicopters, however, it became an expensive habit. When a bull elk put his antler through a helicopter bubble —at a repair cost of approximately $8,000—the firefighters realized that defensive strategy was in order. Temporary corrals were built at some of the helibases to keep the large animals at bay. Other camps used guards instructed to make noise at the approach of an intruder. The helicopters were thus spared any further indignities. Another animal problem was not so simple to solve, however.

The Yellowstone area is known for its bear population, both blacks and grizzlies. Those familiar with bear behavior realized that when firecamps, with thousands of firefighters and their provisions, were established in bear country, certain precautions had to be taken. Since the firefighters were from across the country, most had no experience in dealing with bears. When new firefighters arrived in the camps, they were briefed on the bear situation. Dan Tyres recalled a briefing that he gave to an incoming crew on the Hellroaring fire. "As soon as the crew got off the bus, they circled around me and I gave them a twenty-minute lecture on bears. After I was finished, there was silence, and then they turned to their crew boss. He spoke two or three sentences to them in Spanish and they nodded and marched off. I wondered (with apprehension) how much they really understood."

A number of preventative measures were developed, and all firefighters were instructed to follow them carefully. The proper handling and storage of food and disposal of garbage was a big issue; crews were given pamphlets on travelling in bear country; and firelines and camps were regularly inspected to be sure that these measures were being followed.

Bear came into camp and tore up cook tent...ripped hole to get in and ripped hole to get out... took garbage. Three nights in a row, third night into tent.

Curt Bates, an incident commander on the Clover-Mist fire, related one of his experiences: "A helicopter pilot with whom I was riding received a call from one of the division supervisors who needed assistance with a bear on the fireline. When we arrived, we saw that a grizzly was holding a crew of anxious firefighters at bay along the line. The pilot brought the helicopter in between the grizzly and the humans (they were less than a hundred yards apart) and proceeded to herd the bear off; he finally disappeared over a ridge."

With entire drainages devastated by fire, bears and other animals moved into unburned areas. Not surprisingly, fire camps were also located in these spots. A few startling encounters resulted. Rand Krappral, a strike team leader on the Hellroaring fire, had experiences with bears while working at the Beaver Creek spike camp. "Late one August afternoon, a crew member was manning a pump on a hose line when he saw a cow moose with her calf running in his direction, followed closely by a grizzly. He didn't want to become part of this natural drama and raced immediately toward the nearest climbable tree.

"At this point, the grizzly saw him and headed straight for him. Fortunately, he was able to get up the tree to safety before the bear overtook him. The grizzly, frustrated in this effort, then turned and continued her pursuit of the moose and her calf. In the meantime, the bear's cubs, who had been following at a distance, arrived and were unable to see their mother. Their bawling went unnoticed by the female bear because of the loud pump, but imagining the possibilities, the treed firefighter radioed for help.

Evacuated Slough Creek spike camp because of fire. Evacuated Beaver Creek spike camp because of bear.

"I arrived with two twenty-man crews, and the racket we made encouraged the cubs to move along. All of us then decided to head back to our camp, about three-and-a-half miles away. During the hike back, the sow and her cubs followed us at a distance, and at one point, two of my crew were treed again. We retrieved them and then made it back without further incident.

"That night, we put lanterns all around the camp, and two men patrolled with flashlights. They didn't see anything that night, but the next morning, there were fresh grizzly tracks right through the middle of the camp. During that same night, those bears found a five-gallon plastic container that had been filled with Gatorade during the previous day; one of the crew members had left it in a reservoir by one of the pump stations to cool. When the grizzlies found this, they bit into it and evidently approved, because they proceeded to bite into every plastic container they could locate, including those that held gas and oil. In their quest, they ignored a box of candy bars cached by one of the crew. They seemed to prefer Gatorade to other types of soda. They continued this routine for the next few nights."

CAMPS AND THEIR GARBAGE WERE BEAR MAGNETS.

In many of the spike camps, the crews hung food at least ten feet off the ground to keep it away from the bears. One night, Dan Tyres was camped with a Forest Service firecrew in Hummingbird Basin, a high Absaroka drainage. Earlier that day, they had received a large supply of food, about three times the normal amount, delivered by helicopter. This area had few trees, so Dan, who had brought a horse and a mule with him, decided to stack the food in one spot and tie the horse near it to act as a sentinel throughout the night; Dan had found this tactic effective in the past.

Some of the crewmembers were a little nervous, as at least two of them had been joined by bears for lunch earlier in the day. One large firefighter was exceptionally anxious—he had found a sun-bleached skull and was convinced that it had once been part of a grizzly, and was not entirely convinced by Dan's assertion that it was from a domestic sheep.

Storm Creek camp is becoming a favorite for local bears, an undesirable situation. The remaining two crews and engine strike teams will stay in town.

After an evening of telling bear stories, the crew retired for the night. The anxious firefighter crawled into his sleeping bag, muttering about bears. As the camp settled down, Dan's mule, Molly (a large roan who had been turned out to graze), wandered toward the sleeping men. A curious animal, she had a habit of investigating the camp and its occupants. Walking gingerly among the recumbent firefighters, Molly gently sniffed each person she passed. When she came to the anxious man, who was now soundly asleep, she must have touched him with her nose and it was enough to set off pandemonium. He bolted awake and began shrieking in stark terror. The confused mule couldn't imagine what had caused all the noise, and bolted out of camp. This set off the horse tied near the food cache, and he scrambled and whinnied in fright.

By this time, *everyone* was awake. Some of the men tried to calm down their terror-stricken comrade, while others just tried to figure out what was going on. Before long, they'd all settled down again, and Molly, reassured, slipped back into camp. The incident provided the men with some much-needed comic relief.

FIGHTING FIRES FROM THE AIR

Considering the number of helicopters and planes involved in combating the Yellowstone fire, it is incredible that there weren't more accidents. At one time, there were more than sixty helicopters involved in the firefighting effort. All of the pilots experienced more than one kind of tight situation, and most cited some frightening near-misses with other helicopters. John Keys, an air-support supervisor with twenty years' experience, observed that "it's not one big mistake, but a series of little ones that causes trouble. At one time, I had fourteen helicopters in the air in the same area, and felt that the situation was getting marginal. In an effort to establish a higher degree of safety, I pulled everyone down, modified some of the patterns and frequencies, and sent them back up again."

HELICOPTERS DIPPED WATER FROM LAKES AND RESERVOIRS.

Flying helicopters into the face of fire requires critical judgement and extraordinary skill; ego has no place. If the wind is too high, or the visibility too bad, the helicopter comes down—the pilot's life depends on it. Roger Sadler, a helicopter pilot, noted that "the difference between a good pilot and just an aircraft operator is that a good pilot truly knows his ship; he's one with it, it's an extension of his body that allows him to feel the exact position of the ship and its relationship in space to other objects."

Despite all precautions, accidents did happen. A helicopter pilot working on the Clover-Mist fire near Cooke City was dipping water out of a lake when the cables to his bucket hooked over one of the skids. When he pulled the power to raise the load out of the water, the helicopter's center of gravity shifted and it tipped over and dumped into the lake. The pilot swam to shore and other than a few scratches, only his pride was wounded; the helicopter itself was a total loss.

VERTAL HELICOPTER DROPPING ITS LOAD OF WATER.

Another thing that made helicopter work dangerous was that, most of the time, they were working at full-load capacity, fighting tricky air currents, heat, smoke, and the turbulence created by the fires. Curt Wainwright, who logged 650 hours of flight time, noted, "There were times when, because of poor visibility, I had to stay very low and hover from treetop to treetop just to be able to get my bearings."

Jackson Hole...two persons killed ...helicopter crash, water bucket caught on trees, pulled them to the ground.

To the untrained ear, the voices blend in an indistinguishable chorus, but to the pilot, the radio is his lifeline and he must be able to differentiate the voices and commands so he can visualize where the other helicopters are and what is happening beneath him. Sometimes the news is good, and the pleased assertion "We've got it under control" can be heard. Other times, it's a completely different story.

Pilot Roger Sadler recalled one such situation. "In the Slough Creek drainage, we committed a major operation to the containment of the fire. Thousands of man-hours were spent cutting and hacking a firebreak from the top of the ridge down to the Slough Creek basin. We flew countless hours hauling people and supplies into the tight landing zones, and dumped thousands of gallons of water on the fireline to bring up the moisture levels on the green side. The fire bombers dropped retardant ahead of the fire in an effort to slow it down.

"Finally, the winds were right and a back-fire was started. Midnight brought a wind shift and the fire started burning back toward the fireline. We began flying buckets at daylight and continued all day; Captain Stone was flying N664 and we were rotating out of the same dip point, averaging five-minute round trips with 2,000 pounds of water each trip. The smoke was thick, about a quarter-mile visibility, and it became increasingly difficult to take a deep breath without choking.

"The heat of the fire forced its way into the cockpit—flames were running about 200 feet above the trees. The ground manager gave the word to pull out the ground people to prevent injuries, and over the radio, I could hear the bitter tone in his voice as he admitted defeat to a raging fire with a two-mile front, driven by high winds, roaring down the drainage."

Helicopters were also used extensively to transport fire personnel and supplies from one location to another. It was on one of these occasions that Ken Johnson made a daring rescue on Table Mountain near Yellowstone's southern boundary.

The "20/20" news crew spent the day on the Wolf Lake fire yesterday. They had to be airlifted out when the fire bumped the line in the area they were in.

"A few days earlier, I had flown a couple of firefighters to the top of Table Mountain so they could monitor the local situation. On the day of the rescue, they had radioed in during the morning that they wanted to get off the mountain, but weren't experiencing any particular problems. Since they didn't seem to be threatened, and since helicopter time was at a premium, they weren't scheduled to be picked up immediately. Later in the day, though, they radioed back that fire was closing in on them and they now *needed* to get off the mountain.

"I was dispatched to fly in and get them out. I arrived in the middle of a huge firestorm, with seventy-mile-per-hour winds and heavy smoke. This wasn't a place I wanted to be, but these people had no other way out. With visibility ranging anywhere from one hundred yards down to nothing, I worked my way up the back side of the mountain, next to a cliff; it took me twenty minutes to find a place to land. I wasn't exactly sure where the two people were, and they couldn't hear me land because of the roar of the fire. I sent my helitac person out to find them.

Foot problems continue to be the biggest single medical problem.

PLANES DROPPED LOAD AFTER LOAD OF FIRE RETARDANT.

"The next thing I knew, three- to four-hundred-foot flames jumped right over the helicopter—I thought I was going to have to shut down the machine, bail out, and watch the ship burn; it was a pretty sick feeling. Meanwhile, the firefighters had spotted the helitac (who didn't have a radio) on a nearby ridge, but he didn't see them—then they lost him in the dense smoke. They radioed me, and I sent him back out to the same location and they finally connected and made their way back to the helicopter. The helitac had to carry one of them, the woman, most of the way, and the other firefighter collapsed upon reaching the ship. They were both suffering from smoke inhalation.

"We flew out safely and I returned them to Grant Village, where they were treated and released. I'll remember that pick-up for a long time."

SMOKEJUMPERS HEADED FOR THE PLANES.

SILVERTIP RANCH

On September 3, the Storm Creek fire began to back down the Slough Creek drainage and to threaten the Silvertip Ranch. The ranch (with ten log buildings, most of which were built in the 1920s) was located just north of Yellowstone in the Gallatin National Forest.

Thirty-five firefighters and two fire engines were assigned to protect the ranch. The sixteen ranch employees and about thirty horses and mules were also pressed into service. Sprinkler systems were set up around the ranch complex as well as on some of the buildings' rooftops, trees were trimmed around the ranch buildings, and debris was cleared away. Tension grew as the fire came closer and closer.

About 4 PM, George Jackson, a smokejumper from Missoula, Montana, and another firefighter started a backfire with the hope of slowing down the approaching flames. Meanwhile, two helicopter pilots, Roger Sadler and John Stone, were making bucket drops in and around the ranch. Sadler described the situation from his perspective: "Small fires were spotted at least a half-mile in front of the main fire. We steadily hauled water, but the visibility dropped and the air got hot—it became increasingly difficult to take a deep breath without choking. We made our last trip and dropped on the horse barn, which was starting to smoke; Captain Stone made a drop on the fuel barrels to cool them down. I saw winds filled with fire, tornado-like in appearance, totally surrounding the compound."

An hour later, as strong and erratic winds and dense smoke drove the pilots off, Sadler, after commenting on an estimated 20,000-foot column of smoke, stated that he was returning to the helibase "to stand by for medical evacuation, as I fully expect people to get burned."

The commander said today that he would move horse-drawn plows into Buffalo Butte Flats area and attempt to speed up the line building. This unique approach to modern fireline building is as fast as a cat line and much more environmentally sound.

Captain Stone, in helicopter 664, also reported that the turbulence and smoke were becoming extreme. He radioed Larry Sears, the resource advisor and group leader in charge of protecting Silvertip, that he had "one bad firestorm down there, and there's nothing more I can do for you."

Meanwhile, everyone at the ranch was evacuated to a large, nearby pasture. George Jackson recalled what it was like: "The winds, which were blowing sixty to seventy miles an hour, absolutely amazed me. Embers as large as six inches were falling everywhere. It was so smoky that it blocked out the sun...a very scary situation."

Shortages of water and food continue to be a problem.

Today we lost between 20,000 and 25,000 acres and I witnessed the worst fire behavior of all my fighting career.

Once everyone reached the pasture, all but three people got into their fire shelters. One of these was Sears, who crouched down between the shelters for protection against the wind and also so that he could keep an eye on what was happening; horses and mules, terrified by the approaching fire, were running about, and Sears was concerned for the safety of the people in the shelters. The flames passed to within fifty feet of the group, but no one was hurt. About a half-hour later, the intense burning was over and people began to come out of the shelters. None of the equipment or buildings was lost, a tribute to the firefighters' efforts.

A PHOTOGRAPHERS'-EYE VIEW

Finally, our own most memorable experience came on the afternoon of September 7, when the North Fork fire threatened to overrun Old Faithful. For two days, we had been in the area because fire behavior specialists had predicted that the strong winds were going to push the fire straight toward the geyser, and we wanted to be there to photograph the event, if it indeed happened. We had spent the night at the Old Faithful Inn, and that morning, were informed that the inn was being evacuated. After packing our things, we went outside to see what was happening. Everything appeared to be proceeding in an orderly fashion; park information officers, telling everyone that this was merely a precaution, were directing the movement of the tourists, who were loading baggage in their vehicles or buses.

FIRESTORM THREATENS OLD FAITHFUL INN.

Firefighters were getting ready—a fireline was cleared and sprinkler systems were set up. There were also fire engines standing by to protect the structures. Old Faithful was inundated with representatives of the newsmedia from across the country. Everyone was asking questions, but no one was getting answers—as was frequently the case during this fire season, confusion was the order of the day. About 1 in the afternoon, the wind picked up, as did the smoke columns to the south. A half-hour later, we spoke with a park ranger as we watched two large Vertal helicopters dip water out of a lagoon en route to a fire across a nearby ridge. When we questioned the ranger about the building column of smoke and the situation in general, she responded rather testily that the helicopters had the fires under control.

By 2 PM, the smoke columns were growing larger and getting closer; we were surprised to see that tourists were still being allowed to enter the area. By 3, we were sitting in our car eating a late lunch when we noticed some flames coming over the ridge to the south; it was time to go.

AS THE FIRE CLOSED IN, THE ENTRANCE TO OLD FAITHFUL WAS BARRED.

Gathering up our camera gear, we headed for an observation point that was about a half-mile north of the Old Faithful complex, and less than fifteen minutes later, climbed the last few feet to the rocky outcropping that made up the observation point. We were awe-struck by the sight that spread out before us. To the south, beyond Old Faithful, a billowing mass of smoke that roiled like a monstrous thunderstorm preceded the massive walls of flame heading straight toward the complex. The firestorm produced at least sixty-mile-an-hour winds and a sound that was similar to that of a jet on take-off. Suddenly, the air became dense, filled with ash and the acrid smell of smoke. For a brief moment, our eyes met and we seemed to have the same incredulous thought: "This is really it."

CLEARING A FIRELINE.

Although we had been waiting for the firestorm to hit, we had not imagined it would be like this...I don't honestly know what we *did* expect. Quickly, we looked toward Old Faithful and the inn and our professional instincts overcame our horror as we took as many photographs as we could through the random breaks in the smoke. We were amazed to see a group of tourists, their backs to the flames, waiting for the geyser to erupt. There were photographers and reporters on top of the inn, some of them our friends. What would happen to them? With a terrible sense of helplessness, we watched the spectacle before us; at that point, man seemed insignificant, small, and very vulnerable in the face of the approaching disaster.

The fire was supported by both helicopters and pack strings. Due to limited visibility on most days, helicopters weren't as reliable as pack strings. At one time we had nearly one hundred head of horses and mules assigned to the fire.

FIREFIGHTERS WET DOWN THE HISTORIC OLD FAITHFUL INN IN AN EFFORT TO PREVENT DAMAGE.

The sky constantly changed; huge, rolling black clouds would cover the scene, then the wind would shift and a brief patch of brilliant sky would appear. We watched anxiously as firefighters sprayed the rooftops of the main building to protect them from flying embers. From our vantage point, the tiny streams of water against the backdrop of 200-foot flames seemed pointless.

We were alone on the observation point except for Robert Bower, an Idaho newsman. He had a radio that emitted a constant stream of noise. We became aware of what was apparently the second call directed to our attention: "This is Fire Command, those of you on the look-out point come down immediately, a spot fire is moving in." Stunned by the sight before us, we had missed the first directive. Now we looked around and saw that, to our left and less than 200 yards away, trees had begun torching. The strong winds had carried embers from a half-mile away and a spot fire was rapidly building in our vicinity.

Smoke!!! The acrid smell is everywhere, it burns your eyes and throat—your food even tastes like smoke.

The third call came over the radio, the voice more insistent: "Come down *now*. Don't take the trail, there's a fire on it. Head straight down." With a last look at the Old Faithful Inn, now shrouded in smoke, we turned and began to skid down the side of the mountain; we sprinted through a herd of buffalo who at that moment seemed more menacing than the fires. About half-way down, we could see flames in the inn parking lot and near the cabins. As we continued down, we moved through ever-more dense smoke and flying ash. By the time we got to the level of the inn, we could see firefighters everywhere, their yellow shirts neon in the thick haze, checking for embers and hosing down buildings.

SOME OF THE CABINS BURNED.

Meanwhile, newspeople were running frantically about, stopping to make hurried telephone calls and then dashing off in search of new developments. Someone who didn't know better would have thought they'd wandered into a bandit convention, as everyone had scarves over the lower half of their faces to protect them from the smoke.

This was a very long day.

Hooray, we're going home!

The summer of '88 will go down in history as one of the worst fire seasons of all time. I can't imagine a repeat. But then, the same thing was said about the summer of '86 and then again about '87. If we don't see an unusually heavy amount of moisture this winter, the summer of '89 may be the one to remember.

We felt as though we'd survived a war and it was now time to report to the nation. The firestorm had passed, and the inn and the human population were relatively unscathed. We had to laugh as we watched a park official round up a group of newspeople and herd them across the parking lot so they could film a burning building; it seemed rather anti-climactic after the adventure we'd all just been through.

We had witnessed a historic event, one that held the potential for tragedy but had been successfully survived. We'll remember it for the rest of our lives.

THE HELLROARING SHOW

Toward the end of the fire, Dick Wildman, an outfitter, was working hard to get as much gear out of the camps as he could. When asked how much he'd been able to remove, he answered, "Sixteen tons." This prompted Will Dietzel, situation unit leader, to write the following song, dedicated to the fire crews, overhead, and support crews who worked on the Hellroaring fire.

Chorus: *Sixteen hours and what'd ya' get,*
           A day on the fireline, we're gonna whip it yet!
           St. Peter don't ya' call me cause I can't go,
           I owe my soul to the Hellroaring Show.

Verse: *Out on the fireline, there was an ole' big griz,*
           I'm steppin' lively or he'll give me the biz,
           I'm up a tree, a-settin' in the shade,
           While that ole' griz drinks my Gatorade!

Verse: *If ya' see us comin' better step aside,*
           Many a crew fought it and the overhead tried,
           It was pulaski and shovel from A to E,
           We'll burn it out, then wait and see.

Verse: *On August 15, it started up there,*
           Three days later it was a holy terror,
           Ashes and dust from ten million trees,
           Eighty thousand acres with no birds or bees.

Verse: *The crews and overhead came on the run,*
           Those old firefighters were just havin' fun,
           We'll go back home with the winter snow,
           And think about the fun we had at the Hellroaring Show!

AFTER
THE FIRES WERE OUT

Fire is a necessary element in the natural world. Fire scars on old Douglas fir trees indicate an average frequency of one substantial fire every thirty to sixty years, and park records (kept since 1931) show an average of twenty-two lightning-caused fires per year inside park boundaries. The Yellowstone ecosystem is not only adapted to, but in large part is dependent upon, this force.

THE "RE-GREENING" OF YELLOWSTONE

The environmental segment that most benefits is plant life. With the possible exception of nitrogen, the amount of nutrients available to plants is governed by the soil in which the plants grow. Normally, these nutrients enter the soil through a slow process of decomposition of logs, leaves, and other organic material. Fire speeds up this process, and the resultant ash contains a dense concentration of nutrients. The ash is a sort of natural fertilizer; the minerals and other nutrients are soluble—they do not require further breaking down to be accessible to plants' root systems.

NEW SHOOTS EMERGE FROM THE ASHES.

Seeds normally survive forest fires. In most of Yellowstone, only about one-half an inch or less of the topsoil was burned; underneath this layer, the seed bank was unharmed. The rich medium provided by the ash stimulates rapid plant growth, and the bleak surface of a burned meadow is quickly covered in tender shoots.

Most of the park's old-growth forest provided habitat for a limited number of plant species. Many of those growing on the forest floor are adapted to survive at subsistence level, but their numbers are reduced in time, as they cannot exist infinitely at these low levels. When the forest canopy is destroyed by fire, plants are stimulated by the higher levels of light and nutrients to regerminate and produce more luxuriant growth. Plant communities that spring up immediately after removal of the forest canopy are called pioneer communities, and are an important food source for those higher on the evolutionary chain.

Statistically, when old-growth timber is burned off, total plant species increase thirty-fold within three to twenty years. This in turn results in a greater diversity of animal life within the ecosystem; birds, rodents, and larger mammals have more food and are thus able to increase their numbers. In Yellowstone, biologists and botanists expect plant species to diversify and multiply in the seasons following the fire. Aspen, willow, chokecherry, and wild rose all sprout profusely and are favorites of the wildlife community.

One particular species of coniferous tree is essentially dependent upon fire for its ongoing existence. The lodgepole pine produces two types of cones, one of which opens on maturity and falls to the ground where it lies among downed trees, rocks, and other organic rubble; if seeds from this type of cone do not land in a nurturing environment and take root, they are likely to die or be eaten by rodents and birds. The second type of cone, designated as *serotinous*, only opens at temperatures of 120 degrees Fahrenheit; this temperature is unlikely to be reached without fire. When fire sweeps a lodgepole pine forest, it leaves behind the

DR. WYMAN SCHMIDT INSPECTS BURNED AND UNBURNED SEROTINOUS CONES.

rich ash bed in which seeds from the serotinous cones can quickly germinate and become established. If fire is excluded long enough, a lodgepole pine forest eventually reaches a climax stage and is likely to deteriorate or otherwise change in character.

Streams and other bodies of water also benefit from fire, as runoff from the ash floor feeds and increases in-stream vegetation, and greater amounts of available sunlight raises water temperature and stimulates aquatic productivity. These changes ultimately mean that fish can reproduce themselves in greater numbers.

AFTERMATH: MAMMALS AND BIRDS

The immediate effects of the fires on Yellowstone's bird and mammalian life were not as dreadful as might be imagined. A certain number of small mammals, such as rodents, were lost, although the percentage is felt to be rather minor because many of these animals can burrow beneath the soil and survive the flames passing over them. Biologists observed that most of the birds that died were confined to nests; there are documented reports of burned osprey nests, which were occupied by hatchlings.

The large mammals were less severely affected. Yellowstone biologists found about one hundred dead elk in an area where the Wolf Lake Fire had made a rapid run. In another section crossed by the same fire, they found twenty-two dead elk and three bison carcasses. In this same area, however, the biologists counted more than three hundred elk that had survived the fire. In September, near Cooke City, a black bear was rescued but had to be destroyed because of the damage to its feet. Documented reports of large animals killed by the fires, however, were minimal, particularly considering the large numbers that inhabit the park and surrounding areas.

Surprisingly, most large animals were not overly concerned about the fires. Elk, moose, and bison were seen grazing placidly as trees burned around them, and after the fires had passed through an area, these animals could be found right up to the edge of the burn, and sometimes even lying in the ash, ruminating. One of the incident commanders was amazed at the bisons' reaction to the fires: "I saw buffalo time and time again just move aside as the fires approached them. The fire

would be racing through the trees and all the animals did was step out of the way. . . . I never saw them run or panic because of the fire."

For some species, the fire actually offered encouragement. Raptors in particular seemed to realize that the large smoke columns signalled food; the burned-over fields exposed numerous small rodents, and they were easy prey for the keen-sighted birds. Terry McEneaney, a park biologist, surprised by the number of raptors in the park, commented that "in Yellowstone, where I normally see only two or three ferriginous hawks a year, I counted forty in one day. There were more raptors out there feeding than I ever imagined would be possible after a fire. It was really impressive."

Hawks and owls were also observed in greater-than-normal numbers, as were mountain bluebirds, who were feeding on meadow insects after the fires passed through. Insects are reportedly drawn to the warmth of the burned areas and provide a rich food source for smaller birds and mammals.

In addition to providing a heat source, fire benefits insects in other ways. Some lay their eggs in standing charred trees (the larvae are a feast for woodpeckers), and others take up residence in and under the burned and rotting logs (providing food for deer mice, bears, and a host of birds).

The net result, then, is not a desolate moonscape but a revitalized ecosystem. Many sections of the park's 2.2 million acre preserve show no evidence of the fires, and those that were burned are already energetically restoring themselves. The face of this land will not be identical to its original, but in many ways, will be stronger and more vital. The park's major attractions remain unharmed. Old Faithful, the Grand Canyon of the Yellowstone, Mammoth Terraces: all are intact.

In the aftermath of Yellowstone's red summer, there is a wide range of opinion; to some, the fires were a historical ecological event, while others saw them as both a natural and economic disaster. The firefighting mechanism, according to some, was an operational success, while others hold that it became an inchoate bureaucracy that stumbled under its own weight.

(LEFT) EXHAUSTED FIREFIGHTER WELCOMES THE FIRST SNOWFALL.
(RIGHT) SNOW IS THE ULTIMATE FIREFIGHTER.

These facts are clear, however. The summer of 1988 was the driest in the history of the park. Conditions in this region of Montana were so bad that Governor Schwinden closed the state to recreational use—including boating—for two weeks in September. The enormous quantity of fuel that had accumulated in the predominantly lodgepole pine forests also predicted potential fire problems. As one of the park's fire behavior analysts stated, "The day was going to come when all that downed, dead, bug-killed lodgepole pine was going to ignite and burn, regardless of what we did."

In the early stages, firefighting efforts were hampered by a shortage of crews and air support. At its height, the scale of the fires was so enormous that there was little hope of control; a fire supervisor, Steve Dondero, observed that "we had 9,000 firefighters on the fires, but it wouldn't have mattered if we'd had 50,000—there was no way we were going to put out those fires."

Firefighters, frustrated by the potency of wildfires, often turn their faces to the sky, pinning their hope on nature, as it is usually nature who deserves credit for extinguishing such large conflagrations. An early log book is testimony to this: "We finally got the fires under control and will be breaking camp"; this entry was followed by "Breaking camp was hindered by three inches of rain." So it was with the Yellowstone fires. Relief came with September's first snow, and was finalized as snow continued to fall into the winter months.

The winter following the great Yellowstone fires was still and quiet. The flames and smoke disappeared, as did the 9,000 firefighters, the army, and the marines. The controversy lingers, however, and where one stands largely depends upon one's perspective. As politicians and park service officials continue to examine and re-examine the fire policy, Yellowstone functions as a unique natural laboratory. Few other places on earth offer a similar opportunity to study the ecological implications of fire on wildlife and the landscape. An ocean of research grants will be processed, and the scientific world will focus its attention on the park for years to come.

For the visitor, Yellowstone National Park will continue to be an exciting place to explore, and will provide a rare opportunity to observe the land re-create itself.